Past & Parallel Lives

Poems by Kaya Ortiz

Kaya Ortiz is a queer Filipino poet of in/articulate identities and record-keeper of ancient histories. Kaya hails from the southern islands of Mindanao and lutruwita/Tasmania and is obsessed with the fluidity of borders, memory and time. Their writing has appeared in *Cordite*, *Westerly*, *Australian Poetry Journal*, *Best of Australian Poems 2021* and *After Australia* (Affirm Press 2020), among others. They were honoured to win the 2024 Dorothy Hewett Award with their debut poetry collection, *Past & Parallel Lives*. Kaya lives and writes on unceded Whadjuk Noongar country, where their name means 'hello' in the Noongar language.

Past & Parallel Lives

Poems by Kaya Ortiz

UWA PUBLISHING

First published in 2025 by
UWA Publishing
Crawley, Western Australia 6009
www.uwap.uwa.edu.au

UWAP is an imprint of UWA Publishing
a division of The University of Western Australia

THE UNIVERSITY OF
WESTERN
AUSTRALIA

ISBN: 978-1-76080-298-1

A catalogue record for this
book is available from the
National Library of Australia
NATIONAL
LIBRARY
OF AUSTRALIA

Cover design by Ezara Ortiz
Typeset in Joanna Nova by Lasertype
Printed by Lightning Source

 uwapublishing

CELEBRATING
90 YEARS

Acknowledgement of Country

The poems in this collection were written on Whadjuk Noongar country, Ngunnawal country and Muwinina country. I wish to acknowledge the Traditional Custodians of the lands on which I have lived and worked, and pay my respects to elders past and present. I acknowledge that sovereignty was never ceded, and that I live on unceded country. This always was, always will be Aboriginal land.

For all my past lives and loves
and for everyone who finds a mirror here

CONTENTS

LIKE A PRIZE

They say longing like it's a problem
but you love the longing. The longing teaches you.

It shows you a hallway.
You write poems into it.

Lora Mathis

I rose from my body and went out in search of who I am.

Alejandra Pizarnik (trans. Yvette Siegert)
from 'Paths of the Mirror'

part 1:
requiem

Final Boarding Call

Airplanes fly off the tarmac into night's black mouth. You – a ghost reflected in the glass. Manila is all grey smog / yellow lights / screaming concrete. Last stop on home soil forms a memory like water, fickle and evaporating. Lock its heavy air in your lungs. Vow never to breathe again.

'Call me before you board,' she said. Dial the number on your tiny Nokia phone (later, tomorrow, next year – reread the messages you'll never delete, a salve for memory's scar).

'Is this it?' she asks, her voice heavy.

There is nothing else left to say, but if you had the words: remember nights pouring rain, lying in bed with the cordless landline to your ear for hours? When the battery died you'd text each other goodnight. Or Saturday afternoons at church choir practice, laughing in the empty hallway.

The way your body begs and begs for closeness. The queer ache in her absence, magnified. Holding her hand, you could hear the ocean, constant and familiar as her voice echoing yours, her face mirroring yours.

'I won't say goodbye,' she says. 'Just see you later.'

All your words un/said like shifting sand. Time and space unravelling.

On the plane, your breath fogs up the oval window. The engine's drone is endless, drowns out your grief. Home dwindles down to city lights, disappearing into the dark. Now it drums like a storm through your body – you never thought you'd lose it all but you are,

you're losing it all

and can do nothing, cannot immortalise a moment or yourself, cannot fit a life or a love or a country into a suitcase.

Here it is. Your life fades like passing airplanes in the night. The sea below is invisible and so far out of reach. Yet you begin and end in it, baptising yourself in this loss.

bayan morphs into
girl who is me who is home
— who will I be without?

Migration story

I dream I am flying but

        the plane never lands

I am one month off the plane

        no one calls me by my name

what do you name a body made

        [borderless]

pale and cold in winter

        a bruise dark enough to stain

skin scarred and shrinking

        find the sun's familiar warmth

my first language

        learn silence

[a second skin]

        in lieu of my stinging accent

a tongue catalysing poetry

        the scar   I find and re-open

speaks me into being

        show me a past and a future

but it's all wrong –

        my skin, stuck in time

my skin, stinging in the sun

        grows too tight

I exist in a fading memory

        gold quieting into twilight

I exist in the long summer

        it is daylight until I blink –

I exist everywhere in

        the aftermath of

flux and flight

        my eternal departure

First Contact

Stardate 1101.13 *arrival*

rules for first contact:
breathe in the sharp bush-gum air.
chameleon into fragments –
a mouth turned closed fist.
everything you are is a knife
through water – bury it.

Stardate 1102.8 *public high school*

there is a right way to be in this world:
white, pretty, straight.

you are not wrong yet, just broken
and evaporating.

no one tells you the rules, so you
observe the rituals:

tanning, hair, boys – and try to be
what they want.

Stardate 1106.21 *birthday party*

play the game to fit in, it's easy
"you are only sixteen once" –
only this marred and hungry once.

the girls are all white and beautiful
when they ask if you are gay, lie
through teeth on bleeding tongue.

Stardate 1112.20 *ceremony*

silence is the price you pay.
    it's simple:
    build a time capsule
of this mouth.
preserve a past before
the uprooting.
remember the self
is secondary to language.

the point is fear, and I
have always been afraid.

Distant Origin

B'Elanna Torres (Star Trek: Voyager)

in the vast testimony   of space
        of this strange new world
every vessel   is a barge of the dead
        (heavy with nightmare)

the body a barricade: Torres' fist to the glass
        memory's sudden attack
                & the Klingon call within

                (every atom is a conduit
                for your blood's haunting –
                no escape in the emptiness)

what is the cost   of pain?
                death's mouth   agape
                we are all
        collateral damage for some alien
        god's agenda
                and the universe is harsh
                and surprising

amidst the drift   the alien waste
only the unravelling
        to tether us   at the end
                light's familiar sting
        Captain Janeway, waiting

                (but not in the way I picture it
                not in the way I need)

I am the one left wanting –
          I, too, am split-
                    between
a star in every quadrant
          and home
                    too many lightyears
                              away

Memoir

tita ruth tells stories because   she belongs to them   they

come alive   eating tinola at the kitchen table with us   in

the house apu built   bare hands on bamboo slats   years

ago   my small weight on the slow rot   now   a scar on my

right leg   a piece lodged inside me   another story to belong

to   now   the rain   the wet earth after it   fertile and

lush   i hear the sound of the name i belong to   tomorrow

we say   goodbye   in a month migration or   according to

my passport   homecoming   citizenship inherited from my

mother or   privilege for being born does not yet become me

down by the river rushing water   sings every ghost alive   do

they know me do they know   i belong to them   that i am

leaving them behind   ?

i wait   for the swallow of time   for my mouth to

recede with the tides   let me exchange my stories for silence

my tongue forgets   i belong to it   every language i have is

borrowed   when i leave i give them back   one   word

at   a   time   but the accent stays   i belong to it   /   i

wear another   my father's melanin in   my skin washes away

in saltwater   i drink it in   it belongs to me   permeates

the cells of my body shores shift into borders   silence is my

name   an ache and a prayer   my body a shipwreck   now

only water   a refracted memory   another scar   another

story   to belong to

Ritual one: silence

i.

it always begins in god's house
    a girl
I am blood-flushed skin
      heart-pounding
    girl   girl   girl

here   they teach love sacrifice
so I deny myself   three times

I'm well-versed at it   remember
how the colonisers wrung
     the deity out of us
took our myth and gave us prayer
    the sign of the cross
        ritual   habit
and forgetting

so I deny myself   again

ii.

I follow a rooster's crow
to the other side
of migration.

I am a southern cross,
lights disjointed in the sky:

blue passport
a language I stop speaking
all the hair I cut off
a label
a prayer to the gods gone
silent

I forget the question
but that was to be   expected.

iii.

I make a habit of beginning.

the name in my mouth dissolves nightly
        and I am a memory
        until morning,
                the prayer blooming
                from my skin.

the question demands a sacrifice –
        body / ritual / memory / light

so I quiet.
                I still.

        I wait.

Hindsight

there's things you don't know
how you know, like the meaning
of a word you read only in a book:

occlusion
irreverent
absolution

no one had to teach you.
some questions lead nowhere.

someone holy speaks
from a pulpit.
when you're young
the world is a riddle.

you learned right from wrong
this way: watching, listening
as the stones reveal their secrets
in ripples through the water.

you pluck and gather them,
small treasures.

then you built a fortress
made of stones.
you built a body.

you built a self
around your self.

there's things you know
you don't know.
it eats at you /
strips you /
reveals you.

you sense it somewhere
deep inside, bubbling
burning magma.

you don't know what it is,
all you know is it exists –

the story beneath the story /
the origin of fear.

what are the terrible secrets
swallowing you whole?

what is it
that you don't know
how to say?

On Wednesdays we play [   ]

CHICKEN

round one:
face to face with [   ]
and you full-moon towards her /
she surrenders / you win.

round two:
the white-light touch
of lips / quiet
seconds mouthing by /
eyes wide / you win again.

TRUTH

one shack, three days, no boys allowed.
you, still brown and shiny as a coin to the nine
white pretty bright-starry tight-skin

kite sky-high girls / who are you crushing on
ever had a boyfriend wish there were
boys here girls but you don't / you don't

POKER

no alcohol for drinking
so you strip instead / swallow
hard as bare skin unfolds
her lined stomach
a shoulder blade
the breasts you dare
a glance at / you,
last of all, crowned
queen of the night

DARE

the water shimmers in the dark / light
from the shack illuminates / your naked body
as you follow their glowing / fairy-forms into the cold
lake. for a second, here / you are: pale and moonlit.
is this what they wanted? / then, a rock catches
your foot. you emerge / wet and bleeding.

WEREWOLF

Rules:
the card is marked red —
keep a straight face.
transformation is pain:
you must become your fear.
truth is the secret under your sleeve,
silence your age-old lover.
there are no friends in this game,
only enemies and victims.

NEVER (HAVE I EVER)

you have nothing to confess,
nothing that laps at your feet, begging.
hindsight is all there is,
a finger marking a trail in the glass.
you know now what it all means
but back then it was a guessing-game.
never have I ever, they said
and you took a sip.

purple flannel shirt
buttoned up to the neck / this love precedes / me / soft looks
/ shaking hands / pink blush / brown eyes / i wish myself into
/ a straighter line / pixie cut / dangly earrings / black mascara /
skipping lunch / it works / if forgetting is an answer / and hunger
/ the only question

ripped black skinny jeans
double cuffed at the ankle / my unshaven legs / twenty years old
and still / unravelling / i grow my hair long / shave half of it off
/ a kind of proclamation / see / skin laid bare / see / holes held
together by threads / the fraying edge of a mouth / made perfect
for secrets

oversized denim jacket
stolen out of dad's closet / sleeves down to my fingers / denim
covers curves / i hide / beneath iron-on rainbow patch over
breast pocket / pass it off as a trick / of the light / this is how
i wear / want / no words for it yet / nothing but a wish / a
consequence / a promise

brown timberland boots
rip-offs from target / heavy on my feet / i walk until a blister
forms / and i too am broken in / an old identity thrown out /
with the heels / i try on labels / see what fits / gay / straight /
bisexual / girl / boy / other / i name the line between knowing /
and denial / i call it / home

Uli

[Bisaya, v.: to go home, to restore, to reconcile,
to return, to recover.]

i. go home

I come from [no/every] where
from sea soil sky

from a single breath
an outstretched hand

and i am born anew
        every day

ii. restore

once   the ocean
was an empty basin

my hand   the dipper
        that filled it

I too   belong to water
I too   am made of salt

iii. reconcile

goodbye is the wound I give you
the only mark I leave behind

time will render me a scar
my mouth / the body's oracle

I ask god for healing
all I'm given is forgetting

iv.   **return**

– the possibility implies
I will find what I search for

[   ] is a memory only
I can see and hold

I find a ghost of home
it is like holding a shadow

I am a ghost in my memory
and there is no going back

v.   **recover**

there is a name for
the ache that makes
and remakes me –

     migration trauma / nostalgia
     homesickness / grief
     / bitter longing

time is my only remedy
     I watch an ocean of it
         storm   and   rage

vi.   go home

I have lost   the threads
     that bind me
the earth beneath my feet
    is soft   as cotton
like sweat   I   evaporate

Timescape

in another world, I watch time
-lines cross: camp 80s leotards

and a holographic simulation
on a starship / imagined futures

and I am both pre- and post-
revelation / awaiting a catalyst

Troi is a ranked bridge officer
without a starched blue uniform

(instead: clinging lowcut dresses
to satisfy sexist producers)

but she sees the beating heart
of it all – a gravity-bending

empathy / in her open palm
I am the grain of sand

she splits into two /
kaleidoscope fractures

I make real her lilting voice /
cleaving gaze through a screen

I want to ask her – is the Betazoid
born knowing grief?

is loneliness a human affliction?
is the darkness of space

something you can feel?
(sometimes the universe pulls away

from me until nothing remains
& I gaze into the mirror of my self

& see only a simulacra)
I want to ask her

what longing sounds like –
does it pulse like a beacon

through transdimensional space?
like a holy hail / an undying SOS

I am frozen in time
I want to know if I can be saved

& can she see me / even if I
look away?

There is no god dead to you
only skeleton churches,

hollow halls and the songs
your fingers callus to.

You find no forgiveness here,
no honey, no promised land.

You wander deserts alone, searching
for the one who searches for you –

God? A husband? The devil?
Judas? Jesus? An angel?

Meanwhile, you resist temptation.
Drink red juice from the smallest cup.

In the night, you dream of women –
scourge of your soul, forbidden.

Are you lost, or held captive?
Are you blind, or unseen?

HELL

Hail mary, full of grace
Our lord is with you

1. Spout prayers into holy books.
2. Ask your mother what desire means.
3. Fail to recognise it inside the face of another girl,
   the soft ache of want a dying hymn inside your lungs.

Blessed are you among women
and blessed is the fruit of thy womb

4. Learn love the same way you learn god – unable to look
   her in the eye.
5. Feed desire with shame until you learn what it means to
   burn.
6. Do not give it a name.

Holy mary, mother of god

7. Tell me about fear, about a secret kept hidden while you
   await the rupture.
8. Tell me about blasphemy, the soft touch of an angel. Is it
   holy? Is it holy?
9. Tell me about bloodshed. About pain. What is the cost of
   salvation?
10. Is it worth it?

I look into the mirror and see all my
past selves. peeling silver dissolves
into sepia tone photographs. my apu

is young and I am the opposite of
a memory: I am every rock lining
the baybay. buo. pero ano ang

nomad kun'di cacophonied by
searching? I know only my name.
only the sand clinging to my skin.

every alas-dos sa hapon, umuulan
na naman – du-pi, du-pi, du-pi.
the wet earth is my mother tongue.

I open my mouth to taste it. tatay
breaks the neck of a manok. I listen to
him speak but I do not know the words.

mamaya, tahimik ang gabi. tulog kami
sa floor beneath the kulambo. tonight
I dream of something other than dugo.

I am a thousand years old and sculpted
from soil. I am carved down and made
to float. I grow feet and learn to walk.

walang kuwento kun'di ito. apu's
brown hand lifted to my forehead.
each line the threads I tie around my

limbs. time cracking salt-white through
the seed. another leaf falls into the river.
I close my eyes and wander out to sea.

Un/compassed

NORTH

the lines they draw around you re-
write history / to uncolonise your
body call yourself whole / what
more do you seek / remember
every lost thing: a name is a word
in every language /
a song to call you home

WEST

" " where are you from
what are you what's that
accent what's the origin of
your name are you
american are you [insert
ethnic group here] why are
you so quiet

EAST

chameleon skin / nowhere /
accent from somewhere else
/ looking for   [home /
language / a seed / a grain
of salt / a name : glass.
rain.   ocean.   flooded.]

SOUTH

brown autumn-leaf in the sun /
pale ghost-gum when the cold
comes / let go come back wear my
skin like mirror / forget i was /
barren all the places i have sprung
from / across a border build
bridges / on my tongue this mouth
is home / & all my questions know
no answer

Oath

Iniibig ko ang Pilipinas

I learn home in a classroom
learn patriotism from
a textbook and a song
I learn to love my country

picking at accent-scabs
from the schoolyard in my
scar-tissue mouth, a mother-
tongue I stutter through

but tisay skin drips coconut
milk onto colonised soil
as brown husks burst open
and I – torn apart –

bear the brunt of the fall
float across an ocean
and let my roots
become me

Aking lupang sinilangan

I was born tethered
to the womb, my apu's nose
laying claim to my face
she calls me dupi

after the yearly rain
and I see her as a dirt road
the final landmark to this story
/ a return to the earth

in another country
it is winter
in another country
I am born a ghost

fists clamped around a
memory – I ask for proof that I
exist / I hold my breath
                           and wait

Tahanan ng aking lahi

I was lost once and then
always / I forget who I am
      heavy with english
and my immigrant ways

so I turn this body mirror
hold it up to the light
to catch the sun
who are my people?

(where is
their home?
do they look
like me?)

I say a prayer to christen
the skin / shout my name
into the void so you know
where I come from –

this tongue my only
                    unfurling.

Etymology of paalam

after K Ming Chang

I. *Pa*: a prefix used to let, make, ask or have someone do
   something

    A. Filipino is a language of affixes. tenses born out of
        1. roots and branches. present repeating into future –
        2. the tension between what is un / real
        3. history: still truth beneath the lies painted over it

    B. to season a question, cull a demand into request
        1. a mouth growing smaller while the tongue thickens
        2. sugar-coat teeth until enamel melts away. my syrup
           smile
        3. preceding the words caught behind my teeth

    C. swallow down the stinging
        1. the stories don't translate, don't encode into
           permanence
        2. hunger for what precedes me. go home
        3. to await departure / return. time's oldest ritual
        4. is a flash flood. is night's rapid onset

    D. please
        1. I swallow or am swallowed by
        2. nothing and everything. I beg
        3. to appease the gods. give me
        4. a life I can stomach living

II. Pa: father

   A. speaker of seven languages, he who gives me
      1. my name and a legacy of tongues
      2. a long-awaited prophecy
      3. rebirth / agape / unasked / an answer

   B. our father who art in heaven, hallowed be
      1. the steeple of rejection is
      2. the thorn in my side which means desire
      3. for the love of all that is holy. my body is
      4. a loaf made of stone

III. *Alam*: to know

    A. the world is alien, and you, uprooted
        1. navigating a strange new world of many rules.
           remember
        2. church hall acoustics and your loud voice, shaking.
           what it meant
        3. to be seen inside a spotlight / to be known by a god /
           to love
        4. without understanding

    B. queerness begins in a mirror. the first time
        1.. you google 'am I gay'
        2. you don't pray that shit away. you laugh it off
        3. because none of it is real. you don't even know
        4. how to feel inside your body. let alone

    C. god
        1.. burning bush / voice / myth / spirit / child / mother
           / man / hunger / blood / water
        2. again. I am nothing if not repetition –
        3. I know nothing of

    D. myself
        1. I, a stained-glass façade
        2. the queerness I buried is a seed that grows until I am
           choking
        3. on my own fucking need. I am the lucky one
        4. broken free. the trauma in
        5. the love at my feet

IV. *Paalam*: to let [someone] know

   A. resist the revelation of leaving
      1. school friends find out before my confession, crying
         in the hallway at recess
      2. I imagine nothing is real, and another life
      3. takes shape: here, nothing changes
      4. nothing stays the same

   B. to speak is to make real
      1. god said, "let there be light" and there was
      2. the mythology of the closet – coming out is forever
      3. I am always un / real, my body un / becoming
      4. over and over again

V. *Paalam*: goodbye

    A. a word said over and over
        1. doesn't lose its meaning. it grows heavier
        2. backed by the losses like a landfill
        3. or lighter, when the fear is thrown off at last into the sea
        4. and a name given to itself

    B. I let go of the self –
        1. a retreat I land in, re / created. silence is the gift I gave myself
        2. when the world was ending. but it began again
        3. a new layer of skin over the break, leaving only
        4. a scar

    C. an ending

Line in the sand

there was my voice across a desert,
telling you goodbye.

we built a cathedral of our tears.
cataloguing history, sand lines my palms.

in the stained-glass I witness my life
as painted story, becoming memory

& I would name this ache if it could
tell me what it stands for

but I left the remembering in a dusty
city, & its fingerprints all over me.

part 2:
reincarnation

Wormhole

on the other side of sleep:

only pale hands belong to me

my homeland does not

I speak one language

in circles, searching

but the rip in time has gone

Creation story

i.

brown hands cup water
revealing islands off the deep.
fingers trail the dust –
the first archive is a name
spit out by darkness / born
screaming.

become a god in the act
of creation:
birdsong, raindrum,
riverdance. the water
becomes you
on every shoreline:

what earth can anchor you,
a sea inside a sea?

ii.

my mother's mothers
singing is rain on the
bamboo roof

(something calling to the
soft marrow of my bones)

time is uncharted
and fluid as sleep –

my mother's body was once
my body / threshold of
bloodline memories
& the only earth i knew.

iii.

in destruction everything
is bordered like a map:
earth / body / language / time –

you are named & named again.
evidence of existence
marked on paper
(borrowed name /
borrowed history)

the story's climax
solidifies into present
narratives of colonisation
nothing pre- or post-
anything

(even this re-creation
story / a fabricated
memory of loss) –

iv.

i make home and make it
again,

number the years since i
last returned / heard the name
apu gave me / drank
coconut water at her grave.

try to make something
of a story from
a google search:

"subanen - english dictionary"
"history of subanen in lapuyan"
"people of the river"

or what i create
from a past life:

v.

before rebirth:
trees watched and cradled
your small growing body
watered by the rain
that becomes you

(you were born
not in a place
but a beginning)

in death:
the whole earth becomes
your body
and palm trees grow
around you

dawn of departure /
evening arrival

& history is scattered like
last ritual smoke

Dughan

1. Dughan (dūg-hahn)
   Origin: Bisaya/Cebuano
   Root word: *dugo*, n.: blood
   -*han*, suffix denoting a place
   n.: chest; bosom; heart
   n.: the place I bleed from

2. make a hollow grave
   of my ribcage / a name
   from a hundred countries
   my tongue wraps bandages
   around it, un-stinging
   the bleeding graze / a name
   alive in the storied stain
   left behind

3. I heard it said:
        timuay once ruled this place
        with their land & gold
        & namesake mountains
        & rivers rushing wild
   I heard it said:
        I am descended from the last
        & his children's children
        & the name he gave us all
        & and the faces I wear on mine

4. remember the shock
   & stillness:
   the slow descent of death
   the wound of an open grave.

how the sun becomes a watching
eye above
    a family /
    a country /
    a history
all bandaged in white
to staunch the bleeding

5.   it is a history as old as rivers
   / ocean / sky / rocky shore
   like water it cycles and feeds
   I imagine myself part of the story:
       family as country
       country as blood
       blood as history –
   the tidal flooding
   & seasons of rain

6. what is left behind in
   the tearing away?

7.   Ugat (Ū-gaht)
   Origin: Tagalog/Bisaya
   n.: root
       as in: bloodlines beneath
       the earth
   n.: vein
       as in: that which roots me
       to body and kin

8. the grave will scar over:
   a palm in a coconut grove,
   moss on the river stone
   where the water carves its path.
   I dream them calling my name
   home to the shores of my lineage,
   how I find them in every ocean –
   this too a holy resting place,
   a heartbeat thrumming
   beneath my feet.

Second easter

You sleep a long long time.
Some might even call it death.

When the black years go, you rise
into the light.

No one calls your name.
No one weeps for you but you.

Who crucified you, took your
love and bled it dry?

They would call truth a myth
and miracle, blasphemy.

There are no witnesses
for the wicked,

no home for those who refuse
to rest in stone tombs,

to sacrifice love and life,
        to die.

Ritual two: sacrifice

i.

here   they teach love sacrifice
so i deny myself   three times:

1. all girls get crushes on girls,
   google tells me
2. she doesn't make your heart drum,
   that's just your social anxiety
3. you can't be gay.
   that's it you just can't.

i'm well-versed at it.

ii.

all i have
is prayer

and tumblr in all
its 2011 glory:

blue light keeping
me up late

here, no inscrutable
words from god

but the labels i learn:
pansexual, demisexual

still, i ignore the signs
like i want to kiss a girl

and i forget the question
but that was to be expected

iii.

i make a habit of beginning.

i ask god what it is
        she wants from me:
                every year for seven
                years the same question.

a sacrifice for the answer:
        the crack of my mouth.

Parallel

for Paige Daniels

I am a ghost solidifying into skin again

        when I look at your scars I see a mirror

we are the same shade of etched bloodlines

        you saw it too (or at least I made it so)

like the torn histories of this land and all

        the lands we come from, I see the infinite

ways we are the same: our parallel lives

        meeting in the middle through the

endless crossings of time – will we ever

        meet again or do we just go on

becoming? I can't keep it straight, the past

        before / and the future after

once or someday we arrived like fate

        then or always we departed

on our separate paths

        like we were never here

or we were always here

        under a tree in the park

where we grow our roots

       and my earth meets its water

how I become, for the first time, known

       a secret tender in your hands

raw as confession: our hearts are not flesh

       under a knife and I find no use

for silence / I wanted to fall in love with you

       if only to be known this way

the wind heard it all in my scattering pulse

       you were the first to see me as I was:

brown and bloody and breaking

       you heard my haunted voice from the dark

in that single moment's crossing

       I forget what it means to be alone

& this was the gift you gave me.

Self-insert Trek: Flashback

0. Self-insert as narrator:

[i cannot look you
in the eye / tell the story
without telling it]

       i am in flight again: [ ] is a name unspoken:
   i am creating a home without boxes: [ ] is an extended phase:
      i am rehearsing a memory: [ ] is a re-run
        repeating: i am quietly imploding:

    cascade of stars. awakening.

    [i am something other
    than what i th/ought]

the irony comes after a premature wedding / everything created
is bound by its context /
that is, space and time / so i will forgive myself later / for now,
the next iteration:

1. Self-insert as a story:

Star Trek Voyager is an odyssey – an impossible
& endless homecoming. i start to believe
in impossible feats like survival:
      in the face of destruction & death
       the starship rebuilds itself again.
     the crew renews its memory each episode,
       no trace of the last trauma

[i will remember this later,
post- the edge of my known world
when i excise the boy from my poetry]

2. *Self-insert as Chief Engineer:*

Lieutenant B'Elanna Torres is a mirror:
angry / lost / confused / conflicted / alone

half-Klingon & half-human, B'Elanna
cleaves & falls into herself, a shattered identity

[relate / recognise / reflect / become]

3. *Self-insert as space:*

grow obsessed with a gravity i can't escape / a black-hole anomaly
/ can't get enough / don't realise
i've fallen in love with a fictional character / all that misplaced
longing projected into nightly
viewings:

she sees my pent-up longing, all that stifled ache /
i am begging to be seen / i am guilty for wanting it

what it comes to:
fanfiction is a necessary salve
– i falsify into re-tellings:

#StarTrekVoyager #f/f #Torres/Janeway #Kathryn/B'Elanna
#angst #femslash #lesbians #slow burn

in the blue-lit dark i learn / what i had never known of desire.

4. Self-insert as Captain Janeway:

nothing is simple about confronting fear
when flung into a distant quadrant.   which is to say
at first

                  i looked away
          from [memory / mirror / mouth / monster]
                      or: the answer i seek

5. Self-insert as alien lifeform:

i sleep next to the boy
not with him.

my alien body
my alien longing.

                      6. Self-insert as audience:

            follow the fanfic to its logical conclusion:
          the captain and chief engineer's lusty affair,
                  a hook-up in the Jeffries tubes.
          learn how to pleasure another woman
                  in some far-off impossible
                          future

a fiction twice, three times removed.

[the strangeness of a future where
interspecies relationships are widely accepted,
but two women never fall in love.]

7. Self-insert as a starship:

my body a ship dead in the water.
my body a wreckage in the deep –

number seven searching seasons before i return

    to myself /   ruptured.   reborn.   rebuilding.

Ghost story

(Star Trek: Discovery)

Like U.S.S. Discovery, mythologised. A water droplet on the
cosmos-web, there & then gone. In the wake of the wreckage, one
blinking light to guide you, to open the way. Airplane window
seat in the dead of night, like a shooting star seen from earth. The
image burned in your mind: what you left behind / what you're
leaving now. A mirror like two sides of the moon. Your eternal
departure, battle-scarred. The future was desolate once – you saw
it. You were here, time & time again, locked & tethered. The new
world blooming from the black. The old made & remade many
times over, marooning you to the history of ghost stories. What
is gone & left behind, rusting among the ruins of stars, the bone
& dust of planetary rock. How it haunts you – siren of lost things.
Feel the burning ache of all you want, all the things you cannot
name. Your voice lost to the vacuum of space & your strange
tongue. Remember: the other world, the other self, the face in the
mirror. Everything bent & broken through the rabbit-hole of time.
What you keep alive is what haunts you. At the far ends of the
universe, become what you fear & find that it does not end you.
See the spectre of stars in the endless night, made & remade &
remade again. Gone the way they came.

it's a milk teeth ache.
longing is queer domain –
shut the door with shaking
breath and lies.

the first time is all panic.
every time after is its ghost,
a mercury grip on the fever
fall of her name.

find and rewrite your body
into hiding. sleight of hand
secrets, swipe right like
a rhyme but

the girls always stop texting.
sit with the longing until
your hair turns white,
the eighth deadly sin.

grow wild with it, bone
through bleeding gum.
only one thing stops
the stinging.

try them on until they fit –
    1. queer vernacular
    2. (the word 'queer')
    3. deny desire
    4. queer code your body:

        say the clippers will
save me this time
        the piercing will
save me this time
        say I don't need
the love of a girl.

you will falsify yourself
into mythology but it's
no unguent for shame,
no cure for time's crossing.

this want is glitter-thick
and you are fourteen again,
the future wild as a pride
parade.

in the aftermath, you
are earth-bound,
dropping handfuls of
teeth into dirt.

like a myth they
flower and cleave
again. again.

Like a hyacinth
in the mountains
that shepherds crush underfoot.
    – Sappho (trans. Julia Dubnoff)

1. swipe right on the purple-haired girl
    on tinder
        ~~just~~ a friend
        but she's cute and you're ██████
        she's ██████ / it'll
        never happen

2. notice the girl walking in
    late to class
        underarm hair,
        rainbow earrings
    " she's defo ████ , right? "
    " yeah, but you're ██████ "

3. imagine the end of the world
    and you, never having kissed a girl
    in the lavender light of:
        a bar
        the cinema
        a jacaranda tree at dusk
    melodrama: it's a ████ trait

4. wonder how
    coming out would go –
    " I'm ██████ "
        she loaned you

two books, both by
██████ poets
they're fine with your
██████ cousin, so
why not you too
" I have a ██████████ "

5. become that hyacinth
streak in the sky,
heart-thumping-
a-bruise-into-your-chest,
violet petals crushed
into driveway concrete
purple is the ██████████ *colour*

Broken Pieces

Seven of Nine (Star Trek: Voyager)

there were many before her / but we are always last / and found /
driftwood bodies in celestial sea / she did not ask to be saved / i
did not ask to leave / nebula-fragmented into starlight / Seven of
Nine is cyborg / alien / god / queer / other / her body for the male
gaze / and me / sleep walking still / everything i was forgotten /
we assimilate fist first / learn the world over like constellated sky /
what does it mean to be necessity / abscess / abyss / a closing door
/ an awakening / the closet is a matter of space and time / we hide
and grow into it / lightyears ahead / small bodies full of longing
/ i wait twenty years for her / but they do us no justice / relegate
us to sideways glances / plot points and hints / to final episodes
/ no words no certainty / our bodies suspended and awaiting /
gravity's grip

Binary Stars

Michael Burnham (Star Trek: Discovery)

necessity demands   the stoic Vulcan
exterior   brown skin smooth
as a tritanium hull   [in this way I
am like the one I desire]   the guilty
mutineer   stone cold above the
storm   they would kill her and
justify it   if necessity demands
Burnham has never been in love only
stuck in time   a tongue darting
around a gap   [in this way I am
unlike her: the gap awash with
longing]   later   there is the grip
and the freefall   later   the hand
around her neck   but I imagine it
differently   I resurrect us both:
Sylvia Tilly with her soft white edges
no sacrificial lamb no bloody visions
only locked lips   bright lights and
synthehol   / but this is not how
the story goes   Michael's   or mine
somehow   we are always cursed
by time and all its   iterations

7. you live with it so long it consumes you, a blackhole in your stomach.

13. the world inside your head is a fiction.

17. you see the future, real and still-becoming. as if memory.

9. you see them everywhere, the loves of your life – they don't see you, fighting your own skin for a glimpse of [divine / nebula / hellfire / yourself]

2. in one reality you never left, grow your colours like a callus in all your native tongues.

16. the tragedy and the blessing: all your mirror selves unimaginable.

5. under a tree in a park, the confession claws your throat. the friend who could – in another life – be something more, appears in your dreams years later to hold your hand.

15. you wrench the door open again and again. to the sudden pang of light.

11. the ghostly almosts of loves that scar your heart, starving / surviving.

8. in every corner there are cobweb-threads, iridescent. shadows of alternate timelines crumble when your eyelids flicker.

3. the past is alive and constant, water in cupped hands escaping you again and again.

1. you are there forever in that church hallway, your best friend's laughter echoing in the emptiness. your beating heart drowned out by the singing choir. like angels in heaven.

10. watch it over again: the girl next to you at [   ]. the quiet desperation of your body like a caged dog.

6. it was never about the girl but your hunger.

14. still you wonder if a girl is an answer.

18. the future you see is a past repeating. everything superimposed.
19. you live with it so long it becomes you. a knife drawing its own blood.
12. a million possibilities writhe and grow, a knotted, beating core.
4. the tragedy and the blessing: there will be no forgetting.
20. and always, this: you, here. now.

Ritual three: crisis

      i.

i

     are you a lesbian?

just

     what? no, no way!

have

     there's nothing wrong

one

     with being gay

question

     you know

      ii.

she is the pastor's daughter

perhaps she has never heard the voice of god

she doesn't know until she knows she knows

does this make her a sinner?

only if she says it   out loud

iii.

it is only a matter of time / it is only a matter / of time / it
is time is a matter only / only time / only time is a matter of
/ truth / only truth / matters / what matters / what matters
but the truth / truth is what matters and time uncovers it /
how long? / fourteen / twenty / twenty-five years / it is
only / a matter of / tell the truth / time / truth / it matters

iv.

i ask god what it is
        they want from me.

v.

there are no easy answers:
the open crack of my mouth
is a sacrifice i pull and push
towards / against / towards

vi.

in the beginning
        was   the word –

            god

            girl

            gay

in the beginning:

            [fear]

            [shame]

            [silence]

vii.

and how does it end?
how does it end?
does it end?
does it end?
does it
end?

Timelapse

i wanted / i was

        [not] ready

the ocean / the edge of

        lost

the world / my life

        the unknown

the day we met / & you

        happen[ed]

& i / the sand the water

        imagine

what we could be / come

        i don't even know who i am

like this / ripples in the waves:

        the rest of my life

Habi (Woven)

I am floating down a river

soaked to the skin

a baby in a makeshift sling

my mother

wrapped in a malong

washes her clothes by the rocks

I awake on a woven mat

I awake

and the house is on fire

my body is whole

I am ghost or ancestor

fingers to yellow paper

a descendant pens a letter

my grandparents write

in english

different mother tongues

somewhere it is flooding

letters in a battered suitcase

elsewhere it refuses to rain

water, stone, my bones

a grave in a coconut grove

a faded malong

is an archive

is a record for who?

mum tears a malong in half

another river dries up

the table set for breakfast

I close my eyes and picture

a child in my father's lap

apu

this future for another life

the past unfolding into us

I forget

time is a woven cloth

the Tagalog word for

remembering

everything

is (alalahanin / lahat)

Tasseography

Oras.
Once – tita's iced tea, steam spilling from the tupperware
pitcher's gaping mouth before time cools the burn. Later, she'll
call us in from the street, call the kuyas down to eat, her come ya
kita ringing out in a language I'll never learn. Displaced in time.

Ginto.
Intro to Mandarin, my ate's textbooks under my arm. A girl in the
front row, her skin brown as thirst / a mirror image in gold. The
old tug in my chest, alight – the one I never name but quell again
and again.

Linguahe.
Chavacano is the only Spanish creole language in Asia. Remnants
of colonialism in country, hometown, kin; in a name / a country's
name. The desire to understand – a constant pull against the
desire to forget.

Pinto.
The girl walks in late to class, takes the seat in front of me. The
power of proximity. Later, the tutor calls her by my name and
me by hers. I turn this mistranslation into a door, opened /
unspoken.

Tsaa.
The Filipino word for tea is derived from the Chinese chá. The
Filipino word for aunt is derived from the Spanish tía. Filipino,
from the coloniser's name. My first language, once, was Filipino.
What else survives this othering?

Kami.
She forgets her textbook, climbs over the row of chairs to share
mine, elbow to elbow. The body's loud language of dissolution /
evaporation. Over the din of faltering tones I create this memory
& make it mean something it doesn't.

Puti.
I forget myself, become a tainted tongue and mispronounced
name in a room of white classmates. Grow accustomed to
disappearance, be other or nothing. The ongoing legacy of
whiteness is erasure. Until –

Pulo.
Where did you come from, I want to ask her. How did you get
here? Is your belonging, too, tenuous as twine? To hold my
skin up to hers, trace the lineage of islands. If I speak desire in
another tongue will it make it less real?

Langit.
In the middle of the night, I google which words in her native
tongue match those in Filipino, start a list in my phone. A poetics
of symbolism – our imagined pasts and futures intertwined in
earth / sky / the legacy of tongues.

Mahal.
The tragedy: I [left / lost] before I am [found / fluent /
fed / falsified]. The cost of migration is my body, multiplied.
Amputation makes everything a phantom. In the dregs I make
and remake it:

Inom.

Time constellates memory / there, in the grip of desire, despaired my thirst's nettle / the hole in my tongue & the impossibilities of longing / no matter how I trace the picture, the ending burns my throat / & remains there, an echo –

Assimilation is not my name

a name: ancestor,
a thread i answer
at last —

sister says, what if
they think you are
full-blooded filipino?

spanish surnames
conjure colonies,
at least for us —

    (i have origamied
    a name out
    of shape before

    made my mouth
    a winded thing,
    for who?)

i am still learning
to parse a body
out of theory

let me let go of
the old white lie —
water in blood

    (after all, isn't
    australia also
    a name

enacted,
tacked on like
an afterthought?)

remember: southern
land, white history
erases nothing –

there is still every
before / before
/ before

      (assimilation is
      not my mistaken
      mispronounced

      name is not any
      body's name is not
      whitewashed country)

so i begin with a name:
trace it, coil my tongue,
a river threading

back
back / back
back.

part 3:
revelation

when I look back at the world,
there's the rocky beach
licked clean by saltwater.

inihaw na isda. kinilaw. lato.
tastes of the ocean.

when I look through the water
of memory, this is what I see:

my parents don't let me ride a jeepney.
dad drives us to and from school.

along every street in every city,
black wires thick as hair twist and coil
between concrete poles.

      I don't know what runs through them.

I spend six pesos of my allowance
to buy turon from the canteen.

outside the school gates,
across four lanes of traffic
there's a mall and a McDonalds.

in childhood the world
was just the world.

during wet season, rainwater
awakens the marshlands
sleeping beneath the school.

in the break we'd visit
Lapuyan. never left the house
except to go to church.

Exercise a high degree of caution
when travelling to the Philippines.

Do not travel to central and western
Mindanao, including
the Zamboanga peninsula.

have I told this story before?
how I haven't been back.
how I look at the memory as if
it's underwater:

eight hours in the car.
I'd lie down and stare up
at the sky through the window,
the clouds drifting by.

eight hours on the plane.
I look down through clouds
at the endless blue ocean,
dotted white by waves.

I'll never know what
I would've known
or who I would've been
if we'd stayed.

Sundays of song and scripture and the sin in your skin. Take the god out of the empty sanctuary, find a ghost mapping the years: pinky-promise shades of sunset on a rooftop. New Year's eve fireworks sound like no sleep, the only way to say goodbye. To an old self, to the friends who leave the country and don't come back. The first year of darkness, afterwards. Un-ash all the letters from the wind, so you never lose the paper-trail. In a past life your gutted mouth. The song played over and over. The white scars that time healed, until you curse yourself for forgetting. Find yourself suddenly at an altar, weaving vows. What do you name the haunting loneliness, after? Dreams of a different life take hold, a picture of never ever. But the story goes she fled her hometown, not once but twice, and then crossed a desert to find herself. Where did it begin, the fear of being seen? It's all you want, now. Past the distant forests, the river and mountain. The someday Sundays of eternity look like another life, another self. Preserved in honeyed amber and so full of the future. Beyond borders / beyond time / beyond a body. You didn't leave her behind. Believe in this: the memory is proof you were real, so become your own witness. Take the sorry out now, what do you hear? An existence beyond memory. The forgiveness you give yourself. A promise breaking open, setting every ghost free.

Beyond knowing

i play   the one i'm living

a kind of limbo   beyond

something

i've known
                        i wasn't
        myself

accept   the caveat
        couldn't be
        known

like a knowing beyond knowing

i suppressed
        myself
                / face the
terrified   possibility

all the other ways i[t] could have
[   ]
                        considered
exclusively
                attracted to girls
god damn it

that knowledge

i might be
[   ]
                    beyond

hope   and freedom

i'm finding   self-love

Ritual four: revelation

i speak,

and there   i am.

Origin story

I am from southern islands,
from bamboo borders & the hallowed crossing.
I am from the curved horizon, the sudden
descent of dusk, hazy as smoke.

From hands rough as palm tree bark
& the young green coconuts, fresh as seawater.
I am from my mother's crowded mouth, her crooked
teeth and many accents; from my father's folklore

and five languages. I am from the language of
bloodrush / translation / the song and the gong.
I am from brown salt-skin, the swallowed sun.
From too-good english: script, verse, poem.

From ancient rivers & ocean veins,
a mountain-walled city and my many names.
I am from the culture shock, a mouth too crowded
with language to speak.

From the break, from the heartache,
from the "where are you from?"
I am from the waiting. I am from unlearning
every word for home. I come from

the crashing seas of time, the shores
washed clean. I am borne on the body of my longing.
I am my oldest memory, the first & last of kin.
I am from the roots where every story begins.

Undercut Season

Kitchen scissors to my long black hair, the clippers on the sink.
Outside, jacaranda trees line streets, purple smashed into concrete.
Last full-moon violet night I made out with Rosa Diaz in a dream.
She told me [insert character] is definitely 100% gay and that
I would totally rock an undercut. Hair on the floor, clippers buzz
over Janelle Monáe singing on repeat. My own anthem of liberation.
I am a kind of Disney-animated Mulan, queer and desperate to
[pass / hide / fail]. The ritual is familiar – at seventeen I cut off
all my hair and tried not to stare at two girls just holding hands.
Now my past falls into the sink, confettis the floor around me. The
back of my head is black fuzzy velcro and I run my hands over and
over it. The scars on my arm are just that, scars. Someday I'll watch
movies with the girl I like. She smells like lavender ice cream, and
I'll write her a poem of all my purple-stained joy. But for now I
put the clippers down, brush sharp hairs from my neck. Jacaranda
undercut season: how I practice shedding shame again and again,
until the needle stops spinning. How euphoria grows when you
follow joy, the brightest of all the colours.

Masc.

big dyke energy. stone butch sweetness. double salt liquorice. chicken breast tender. trucker's tan realness. real reckless. I'm real real.

little spoon. little bitch. dark and brooding. daydream drifter. butter yellow. touch me touch me. pillar of warmth. boob pillow baby. I'm real real.

paper-cut fingertips. steel-toe stubborn. off with the fairies. cottagecore lumberjack. escapism artist. you moonlit magic. rivers curling swift. and I'm real real.

typhoon power. home is a heartbeat. louder louder. cruise controlled laughter. peach-skin bruising. don't bleed lightly. stone holding water. water holding water.

transcend the mystery. contradictory.
it means nothing / it means everything.

A mirror soft as water

Was shame always our
inheritance? Rite of passage,
not one we chose but what
was given to us long ago

like a bottle to tend the wound.
I read *Stone Butch Blues*
looking for a mirror. Instead
I find a knife-carved scar,

all the blood they shed for
this – my own mundane life.
The love we'd risk it all for:
to see the body in the mirror

un/bound, un/broken.
To love the woman in your bed
and know you were made for this.
To fight the whole world for

a glimpse of another,
turn the yearning into hope
of what's to come. That death
will not always become us.

And here we are: watching
two women kiss in the dark
on a television show set in
1940s America. We cheer

for representation and weep
knowing happily ever after
is not guaranteed. Await
the gut-wrenching revelations

of being, the story set in stone.
I let it haunt me, everything
we lost to get here. Still
it breaks me glass-door open,

the ways we find each other
in mirror upon mirrored reflection.
Because after all I was not alone.
After and in spite of it all.

Sa kabilang mundo

what do I know of legacy? they do not lay siege to
remembrance our names
a mouth inked in smoke, I am green as
worlds fingering the dream-dust the moss-soft riverstone

what was surrendered to the water a word
sharpens when the thunder calls its harmony hum
elegies return to the sky I go with them
until a song is just a song calling, calling

what can survive the violence of grief blown into
ships, the breeding darkness? the wind like ashes
in the glass, a blur of light a palmful of seeds
in the light, a revelation in child hands

what is blood without earth? I live a thousand lives
a body released from gravity a hundred thousand lives
calls a chasm its home in this one in this one in this
I am only what is given to me I am alive and alive and alive

Bisdak
Ode to Bisaya

you hard-backed jargon, gargantuan
loud-mouth thick-skin not-a-dialect
language in your own right –
you the people's tongue,
forbidden vernacular of private schools
whose curriculum favours english
you worth the peso penalty in the jar

you i learn on the streets, playing
patintero / langit lupa / marco polo
you i hold in my ears, waiting
you language of my youth,
i return to you again & again:
          ikaw samad sa tuhod, hapdos
          ikaw gugma sa amiga, tibuok

you: first, second, third, fourth language
in all the people's mouths
you relegated unworthy of national
language status
you rightful anger drawn out –
          YOU SHOUT
you forgive how the poet falls short.

you stickier than latik on my fingers
you rival to my every spoken word
you knife-sharp against my english-
twisted tongue
you returning with a vengeance,
without warning,
you who grew me –

Uli, *epilogue*

on the plane I eat & sleep
number the years –
seven? six? – since last
departure / final boarding call:

      window seat / fading lights
      the black ocean beneath
      the emptying night
      then / nothing

now I drift & wait for landing
speak / quiet / listen /
imagine my withered voice
cold & buried, lost

in sprawling sentences,
aussie slang. mourn forgotten
filipino phrases, regret
my timid tongue.

at tita ruth's house, a reunion:
cousins, titas and titos
gather over pancit, humba,
tinola & rice.

dessert: the durian uncle ken
brings for us to eat, the easy
giving of flesh soft and yellow,
pungent as the voice I find

in manong jun's stories:
home told in tagalog / bisaya
/ chavacano / subanen –
branches of our history

proof that a root can take
hold anywhere and bloom.
like my own resurrected mouth
open and taking it in –

the guttural remembering
of my body –
the tongue's weight
inside my mouth airborne.

then the sound of my voice
is something I recognise
from a past life: rebirth
& then baptism.

I had imagined my return
a search for marrow,
the harrowed sifting through soil
for a scattering of seeds,

solidity eroded by water-time.
in its place I am made and
found again. I see myself clear
at last – rhizomatic, rooted.

Naming ceremony

i am named for the rain in the old tongue
        i am named for the river
                on my great-grandfather's land
i was plucked from the soil like a seed
        brown and sprouting
                in the sun's familiar gleam
long finger of country pricked with a needle
        to get to the blood where
                the stories live: peace-time, migration
        invasion, diaspora
                the one about the holy book
                ours, the old rituals
                the drought and the flood and fire
  the mountains too remember everything:
        there was the linger of country in a look
                every story becomes prophecy –
                        wetheyi give it all ourmytheir names
i carry them all in the dip of my nose,
        the melanin blooming from my skin
history stirs
i whisper it awake with the sound
        of a name: mine
                dreams are a well of prophecies
                        the land i walk
                        a memory
                my ancestors do not know
                        my name
                dreams are an ocean of memories
                        i dream-remember them all
                        our everything bound together

i will touch the ocean floor
with my fingertips
for the first time
i will understand the words

Dagat

first language ko ang tubig
– dagat
    dripping
       down
           my chin
   asin on skin:
      walang wound
      walang sting

i hear my name
for the first time:
   kaya
   kayang-kaya
   kakayanin
   kinaya
sinabi nila
kaya mo 'yan

    (binigyan ako ng
       pangalan)

   . . .

sa ibang bansa
   i sing hymns
      say a prayer
stay out of the sun
   salt and sweat
      guzzle tubig
tapak on echoes and ruins

mixed girl talks
    kasamang accent
    ang dila galing
        sa past tense
lumalamig
    ang silence –

kasi the translations
    make no sense
i leave myself
    hanging
walang wika
    save this slanging

    . . .

mahirap ang
    kalilimutan
every language turns to lupa
    back to langit or
        kaluluwa

ang dagat, malalim
may nakatago
    sa dilim

mourn the loss:
    no language
    no self

so swallow
     down
     each
     salita
kahit na maalat
sa dila

tubig at asin
     language
     medicine

Pray for us now and at the hour of our death

1. Baptise yourself in water.
2. Kneel before the door and wait.
3. Drink the wine and ask for redemption.
   Or pray and pray for heaven.

Hail mary, full of grace

4. Lose it all in the heresy of your being.
   There will be nothing left to rebuild.
5. What remains in the dark: you and your body and your life.
6. On earth as it is in heaven.

Our lord is with you

7. Hold her hand like rosary beads, an answered prayer in the dark.

Third easter

You open your eyes to
her, waiting.

She knows you and you her,
flesh of your sinful flesh.

You have waited a lifetime
to be found.

She is cracking light, divine,
and holiness is the song

your fingers play across her skin,
her love the sea you walk on.

You have waited for a miracle
and it is the prismed sun,

your resurrection and freedom
her depths of fire, heavenly host.

Drink it in, the sweetest honey
                        and live.

Re/joining

Jadzia Dax (Star Trek: Deep Space Nine)

i.   Join

once, Dax existed here –
another body, another time

antecedent:
    self
    love
    life

turns out you can't
outrun what you want: the life
you could've / should've had
dissects you, leaves a fissure

through the core of you –

ii.   Joining

bear the whole weight of
who you are now:

    Dax's fearful longing
    dreams that belong
    to another self

    (all of it ages old
    yet fresh as time)

every life is a new life:
all this love you hold? never again
for another

it lives in the past

& your longing burrows
lifetimes deep.

iii.　Rejoining

it all returns swift and singing.
you can let go

but forgetting is
the opposite of immortality –

this is why recurrence is
forbidden.

you know the consequences.
it will never come around again

& your eyes are wide open now.
all seven lifetimes wide –

you see the whole universe
stretching out / you with her

& how it never
ever ends.

Past is Present

for Jen Maxwell

Blue July. Cruising in her Commodore through Perth's CBD, you end up in King's Park. In the back of her mind, the first time: you, her, making out behind the trees & blanketed by night.   [How she'd almost gone home. You were parked by your apartment building, hand on the car door. But then: an admission, yours, and all your pent-up longing in a kiss, the years of waiting. She tasted your bittersweet confession and saw you. Met you in your labyrinth of want.]   Now, in the cooling sun, you lie half-asleep in her car, a hand in her pocket. Taylor Swift folk songs lullaby you as trees sway outside the window, watching. You wish you were born knowing everything. Your secrets are the heaviest knowing, knees buckling beneath their weight. The girl beside you is a question your body can't answer yet. But inside the unsaid you are still as real as what scarred you. Repetition, like breathing, is a kind of remembering – you remind yourself of truth each time you kiss her, when the backseat of her car becomes a temple in the dark. Resist the shame of your body's own knowing, the old trauma of holiness. There are a hundred withering ways this could end. You are 25 and know nothing but goodbyes. Stop thinking about deathbeds and regrets. Here, now, is everything you'd ever wanted and didn't have to die for.   Suddenly: she calls you back from the depths, pulls you close until your lips touch.   Here is everything you thought you'd forgotten, every ending you survived haunting you. How, unknowing, they led you here. To a beckoning beginning.

Time Loop
after Maggie Millner

1.

at the beginning of it all was a crossroads –
on the drive home at 3am, something stood

just beyond the headlights' glare.
I have been here before –

I saw the child I was, uncrushed.
then I saw the girl: masked faces of love

& madness. I saw the ghost I had been,
& I saw the road not taken.

2.

I dreamed, again & again, of glass elevators rushing upwards
like a tsunami. my dream-body cowered in a corner, eyes wide
open. outside was a world beyond my reach. inside were the
walls of my fear, the inevitable devastating fall. all this time I had
sensed it coming, a tremble beneath the sand of my life. my life
foreshadowing its own future. & all I could do was watch.

3.

at the crossroads was
an end / a beginning.

I drive home from my
girlfriend's house at 3am

night after night.
fluorescent tunnel lights

pierce my eyes like
a cruel optical illusion,

a gate I pass through
into my old life. I climb

into a bed where another
body sleeps, & press

my body against the smallest
edge of the bed.

4.

past midnight, it is the end of everything. a glance in the
rear-view mirror, & my past lives – once cleaved into epochs of
befores & afters – merge into one. suddenly the road that led me
here is clear as glass. my bruised hands, my shuddering heart, my
life. oh god, my whole queer life.

5.

it was only a moment
then the glass shattered.

but in the shattered glass
lay a hundred refracted

colours, & all my wondrous
selves looking back at me.

Glossary and Translations

from 'Final Boarding Call'

bayan   country

from 'Roots'

baybay	shoreline
buo	whole
pero ano ang nomad, kun'di…	but what is a nomad, if not…
alas-dos sa hapon	2 o'clock in the afternoon
umuulan na naman	it rains again
tatay	father
manok	chicken
mamaya, tahimik ang gabi	later, the night's silence
tulog kami sa floor	we sleep on the floor
kulambo	mosquito net
dugo	blood
walang kuwento kun'di ito	no other story but this one

from 'Oath'

[Note: The poem's subtitles are taken from the first three lines of the Panatang Makabayan, or Philippine Patriotic Oath:]

Iniibig ko ang Pilipinas	I love the Philippines
Aking lupang sinilangan	The land of my birth
Tahanan ng aking lahi	The home of my people
tisay	Shortened form of 'mestiza' – mixed race

from 'Tasseography'
[Note: the subtitles of this poem uses Filipino loanwords or shared vocabulary from Spanish, Hokkien (Chinese) and Bahasa Indonesia, and are translated according to their usage in Filipino.]

oras	time
ate	honorific for older sister
ginto	gold, golden
linguahe	language
pinto	door
tsaa	tea
kami	us
puti	white
pulo	island
langit	sky, heaven
mahal	v.: love; adj.: expensive
inom	to drink

from 'Memoir'

inihaw na isda	grilled fish
kinilaw	raw seafood dish
lato	edible seaweed (sea grapes)
turon	deep fried banana in a spring roll wrapper

from 'Sa kabilang mundo'

Sa kabilang mundo	in another world

from 'Bisdak'

ikaw samad sa tuhod, hapdos	you, bleeding graze on my knees, stinging
ikaw gugma sa amiga, tibuok	you, the love of my friends, whole
latik	caramelised coconut milk

from 'Dagat'

tubig	water
dagat	ocean
asin	salt
walang wound / walang sting	no wound / no sting
kaya	v.: to be able
sinabi nila / kaya mo 'yan	they said you can do it

binigyan ako ng pangalan	I was given a name
sa ibang bansa	in another country
tapak	tread, footstep
kasamang accent	with an accent
ang dila galing sa past tense	a tongue from the past tense
lumalamig ang silence	growing cold, this silence
kasi	because
walang wika	no language
mahirap ang kalilimutan	forgetting is difficult
lupa	earth, dirt
langit	sky, heaven
kaluluwa	soul, spirit
ang dagat, malalim	the ocean's endless depth
may nakatago / sa dilim	something lurks hidden in the dark
salita	word, spoken speech
kahit na maalat / sa dila	despite the salt-sting on your tongue
tubig at asin	water and salt

NOTES

Earlier versions of the 'Ritual' suite and the poem 'Undercut Season' were written during a 10-week hot desk fellowship at the Centre for Stories (Perth) in 2019 under the 'Inclusion Matters' program, and later published in the anthology *To Hold The Clouds* (Centre for Stories 2020).

'On Wednesdays we play [   ]' appeared in *Westerly* 65.1 (2020) and was written during my time in *Westerly's* Writers' Development Program in 2019.

'Mask' was originally published as 'closeted' in *Not Very Quiet*, Issue 4 (2019).

An earlier version of 'Uli' was first published in *Cicerone Journal* (Issue 1 2018).

Earlier versions of 'Distant Origin', 'Timescape' and 'Binary Stars' were originally published online as one poem, under the title 'Strange New Worlds' in *FreezeRay Poetry* (2020).

'HELL' and 'HEAVEN' were written after Arielle Cottingham's poem 'Tramlines' in their book *Black and ropy* (Pitt St Poetry, 2017).

'Roots' was commissioned by the Emerging Writers' Festival 2019 in partnership with *Australian Multilingual Writing Project*, and appeared digitally on YouTube in '#EWF19: The Future of Language.'

'Oath' was first published online by *Djed Press* (2019).

'Etymology of paalam' is written after K Ming Chang's poem 'Etymology of butch', which I encountered through Safia Elhillo's Imagined Vocabularies workshop readings. This poem was shortlisted for the 68th Blake Poetry Prize (2024).

An earlier version of 'Dughan' was first published by be:longing (2019).

'Self-insert Trek: Flashback' appeared in Cordite 110: POP (2023).

'Ghost story' was written for Perth Festival of Literature & Ideas 2023, in partnership with Westerly, and was published in a Westerly online special issue 'djinda' (November 2023). This poem was influenced by Kenji C. Liu's poem 'Migration: Like Paul Atreides', which I first encountered in a workshop with Andrew Sutherland, and Madison Godfrey's poem 'Child of the Hurricane' in their book Dress Rehearsals (Allen & Unwin 2023).

'[REDACTED]' was published online in Scum (2020).

'Habi (Woven)' was written in response to a 'Stories from the Future' workshop run by Diversity Arts Australia, and published online in Peril (2020). The title comes from an art series by the same name, created by Ezara Ortiz in 2020.

'Assimilation is not my name' was first published online by Pulch (2020) and later featured in Best of Australian Poems 2021 (Australian Poetry 2021).

An earlier version of 'Origin story' first appeared in be:longing (2018).

An earlier version of 'Naming ceremony' was published in Cordite 104: KIN (2022).

'Sa kabilang mundo' was first published online by Pulch (2020).

An earlier version of 'Dagat' was published in *Australian Multilingual Writing Project* (2019).

'Time Loop' was written after Maggie Millner's poems 'Proem' and '3.10' – which I first encountered through Andrew Sutherland's Instagram stories.

Acknowledgements

I thank the editors and journals that have published the past and parallel lives of several of the poems in this collection: be:longing mag, Cicerone Journal, Not Very Quiet, Australian Multilingual Writing Project, Djed Press, Peril, Scum, Freezeray Poetry, Pulch, Cordite, and Westerly. Thank you for giving my poems a home.

Thank you to the poetry slams and open mics that held space for my emerging voice: Silver Words Hobart, Canberra Slamboree, Spoken Word Perth, and Perth Poetry Club.

To the organisations who have been a big part of my growth as a writer and the development of this collection: Centre for Stories (especially the 2022 Writers Fellowship), WA Poets Inc. Emerging Writers Program, Westerly Writers Development Program, and Sweatshop Western Sydney. Thank you for your invaluable support!

And of course, to the UWAP team and the Dorothy Hewett Award 2024 judges, thank you, with all my heart, for believing in this book and bringing it to life.

Thank you to the wonderful poets and writers who have mentored, inspired, and encouraged me: Eunice Andrada, Scott-Patrick Mitchell, Madison Godfrey, Robert Wood, Rashida Murphy, Andrew Sutherland, Norman Erikson Pasaribu, Luoyang Chen, Lakshmi Kanchi, Alan Fyfe, Bron Bateman, Mags Webster, Renee Pettitt-Schipp, Daniel Juckes, Kate Noske and so many more. Thank you, thank you for your rivers of words and wisdom.

To my sister and lifelong best friend, Ezara Ortiz – all our lives we have sung, drawn, laughed and told stories together. Nothing is more special to me than having your artwork on the cover of this book. Thank you a million times.

To my parents, Tracy and Joel Ortiz – words are not enough. For your unending love and support, for giving me roots and wings and a name with a beating heart. For my grandparents, Kay and Laurie Priest, for nurturing my creativity when I needed it most, for loving me always. Thank you, I love you all so much.

And finally, for Jen Maxwell – ilaw ng buhay ko – without whom this book would not exist. Thank you for being my sounding board and my gentlest critic. Most of all, thank you for pulling me out of an alternate timeline into this one full of light. Mahal na mahal kita.